STARK LIBRARY

MAR - - 2023

DISCARD

T4-ADM-063

# FREE VERSE POEMS

By Ruthie Van Oosbree  Poems by Lauren Kukla

**Big Buddy Books**

An Imprint of Abdo Publishing
abdobooks.com

# abdobooks.com

Published by Abdo Publishing, a division of ABDO, PO Box 398166, Minneapolis, Minnesota 55439. Copyright © 2023 by Abdo Consulting Group, Inc. International copyrights reserved in all countries. No part of this book may be reproduced in any form without written permission from the publisher. Big Buddy Books™ is a trademark and logo of Abdo Publishing.

Printed in the United States of America, North Mankato, Minnesota
052022
092022

Design: Emily O'Malley, Mighty Media, Inc.
Production: Mighty Media, Inc.
Editor: Jessica Rusick
Cover Photograph: PeopleImages/iStockphoto
Interior Photographs: Africa Studio/Shutterstock Images, p. 5; Amorn Suriyan/iStockphoto, p. 23; Arthur-studio10/Shutterstock Images, p. 17; Artiste2d3d/Shutterstock Images, p. 6; CasarsaGuru/iStockphoto, p. 13; DIGIcal/iStockphoto, p. 11; Evikka/Shutterstock Images, p. 25 (pen); FotoRequest/Shutterstock Images, p. 15 (bluebird); GoodStudio/Shutterstock Images, p. 7 (children); Image bug/Shutterstock Images, p. 29; Just dance/Shutterstock Images, p. 25 (girl); KingVector/Shutterstock Images, p. 19; Korneeva Kristina/Shutterstock Images, p. 24; kotoffei/Shutterstock Images, p. 14; Maria.K/Shutterstock Images, p. 21 (snowflakes); Olaf Simon/Shutterstock Images, p. 15 (tulips); Oleh Markov/Shutterstock Images, p. 7 (road); ONYXprj/Shutterstock Images, p. 18; Petr Jilek/Shutterstock Images, p. 21 (sled); Wavebreakmedia/iStockphoto, p. 9; YUCALORA/Shutterstock Images, p. 27
Design Elements: mhatzapa/Shutterstock Images (paper doodles); Mighty Media, Inc. (backgrounds)

Library of Congress Control Number: 2021953304

**Publisher's Cataloging-in-Publication Data**
Names: Van Oosbree, Ruthie; Kukla, Lauren, authors.
Title: Free verse poems / by Ruthie Van Oosbree and Lauren Kukla
Description: Minneapolis, Minnesota : Abdo Publishing, 2023 | Series: Poetry power | Includes online resources and index.
Identifiers: ISBN 9781532198939 (lib. bdg.) | ISBN 9781098272869 (ebook)
Subjects: LCSH: Poetry--Juvenile literature. | Poetry and children--Juvenile literature. | Free verse--Juvenile literature. | Rhyme--Juvenile literature.
Classification: DDC 821.0--dc23

# CONTENTS

| | |
|---|---|
| Free Verse Poems | 4 |
| Writing without Rules | 8 |
| Nature Free Verse | 12 |
| Funny Free Verse | 16 |
| Action Free Verse | 20 |
| Object Free Verse | 22 |
| Animal Free Verse | 26 |
| Sharing Your Free Verse Poem | 28 |
| Glossary | 30 |
| Online Resources | 31 |
| Index | 32 |

# FREE VERSE POEMS

Free verse poems do not have rules. They do not have to **rhyme**. The lines can be long or short. They may be broken into **stanzas** of any length.

Today, free verse poetry is among the most common forms of poetry published.

Free verse poetry became popular in the late 1800s and early 1900s. Walt Whitman was a famous American free verse poet. He lived in the 1800s. Much of Whitman's poetry is about nature.

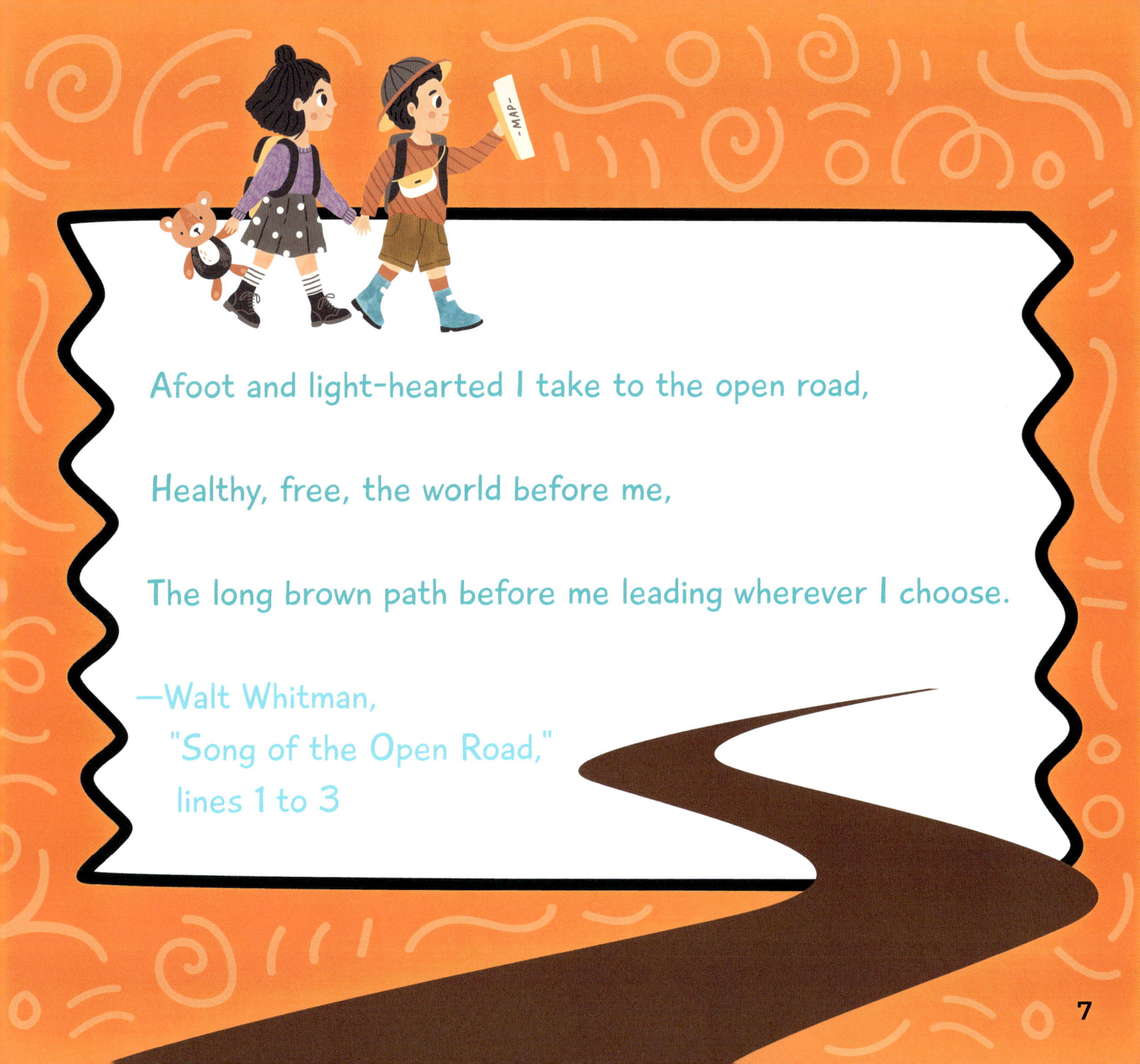

Afoot and light-hearted I take to the open road,

Healthy, free, the world before me,

The long brown path before me leading wherever I choose.

—Walt Whitman,
   "Song of the Open Road,"
     lines 1 to 3

# WRITING WITHOUT RULES

Free verse poetry doesn't have to fit a particular form. For example, you can add **line breaks** wherever you want. You might add one where a person speaking would naturally pause. Line breaks can also create unusual pauses. This can **highlight** important words and ideas.

Write in whatever form helps get your meaning across.

You may want your poem to make readers feel calm or excited. Word choice can help create these effects.

Use short, choppy words for an exciting feel. Use longer, softer words for a relaxed or serious poem.

# NATURE FREE VERSE

Nature is a great subject for free verse poetry. Go outside and observe your surroundings. Choose a subject that inspires you, such as a tree or river.

Observe this part of nature with your five senses. Write down words that describe your topic.

Pick your favorite spot in nature. Write your poem there!

Poets often use nature **metaphors** and **similes**. Think about ways things in nature relate to life. A storm could be a metaphor for a difficult time. A sturdy tree is like a person who takes care of you.

# SPRING

In winter,

everything is quiet.

Everything waits.

But soon,

the bluebirds sing "good morning!"

Emerald ferns unroll from their winter beds.

Soft pink tulips pop out of their cozy bulbs.

In spring,

everything wakes up.

Everything grows.

# FUNNY FREE VERSE

Choose a funny topic for a free verse poem. It could be something that happened to you and your friends. Or it can include characters you make up.

## TIPS & TRICKS

Free verse poems can **rhyme**. Breaking the rhyme can **highlight** words or add humor.

Unexpected endings to a poem can be funny. So can unlikely pairs or silly situations. For example, you could write about a clown attending a boring meeting. You could also write about talking animals. You might even write your poem based on a **pun**!

# THE FROG AND THE FLY

A frog and a fly got on a bus
to get a bite to eat
but the bus broke down outside of town
and left them on the street.

As they began their long walk back
the fly began to moan,
"I'm sick of all this walking.
Are we almost home?

"My wings are tired, my feet are sore,
I'm in an awful mood.
I'm also very hungry.
Did you bring any food?"

The frog said, "I am hungry too!
But I have a trick that works!
I eat whatever bugs me,"
and he stuck his tongue out—SLURP!

# ACTION FREE VERSE

Write a poem about an exciting activity. This could be playing a sport or riding a roller coaster.

Try using **onomatopoeia** to describe how the activity sounds. *Boom*, *pow*, and *crash* are examples of onomatopoeia.

## SLEDDING

WHOOSH!

My red sled flies,

SCRAPING over snow

as I race down the hill.

I'm a rocket,

an airplane.

Nothing can slow me down!

Wait, what's that up ahead?

A lump a hump a bump?

A jump.

Uh-oh.

CRASH!

# OBJECT FREE VERSE

Write a poem about an object. Use your senses to describe the object. Try to paint a picture with your words. What does the object remind you of? Compare the object to these things in your poem.

**TIPS & TRICKS**

Free verse poems can look however you want! Experiment with interesting formats.

Try writing about a toy or other favorite object.

Try using **personification** in your poem. Consider what the object would say or how it would act. For example, you could say a vase is proudly showing off its flowers.

## DEAR DIARY

Each page a
>day.

Each day a
>story.

I spill my secrets onto your blue-lined paper
>in words
>
>in pictures.

And you listen:
>guarding each secret.
>
>Keeping each promise.

My patient, silent, loyal listener.

# ANIMAL FREE VERSE

Animals are great poetry subjects. Choose words that reflect the animal. You might use short words when writing about a squirrel. You could use longer words for a sloth. Use **personification** to describe the animal's thoughts. What would it say if it could talk?

## OCTOPUS

Who needs bones

when you have eight legs,

each with a mind of its own?

I zoom through the water on liquid jets

searching for a lobster lunch

or a shrimp snack.

Yum!

# SHARING YOUR FREE VERSE POEM

Your poem may include **onomatopoeia**. Or it may use words that make the poem feel fast or slow. You can **highlight** those **techniques** by reading your poem aloud.

Free verse poems can also be shared on paper or online. This lets readers see unusual **line breaks** and **stanzas**.

# GLOSSARY

**highlight**—to call attention to something.

**line break**—the end of one line of poetry and beginning of the next line.

**metaphor**—a comparison made by using one thing in place of another or by saying one thing is something else.

**onomatopoeia**—words that make the sound they refer to when spoken.

**personification**—describing an object or animal as though it has human-like abilities.

**pun**—a joke that uses one word to suggest multiple meanings.

**rhyme**—to end with the same sound as another word.

**simile**—a comparison made using the words *like* or *as*.

**stanza**—a group of lines in a poem.

**technique** (tehk-NEEK)—a method or style in which something is done.

## ONLINE RESOURCES

To learn more about free verse poems, please visit **abdobooklinks.com** or scan this QR code. These links are routinely monitored and updated to provide the most current information available.

# INDEX

action, 20, 21
animals, 15, 18, 19, 26, 27

feelings, 10, 11, 26
funny things, 16, 17, 18, 19

lines, 4, 8, 28

metaphors, 14

nature, 6, 12, 13, 14, 15, 26, 27

onomatopoeia, 20, 28

personification, 24, 26
puns, 18

rhyming, 4, 16
rules, 4, 8

senses, 12, 22
sharing, 28, 29
similes, 14
stanzas, 4, 28

Whitman, Walt, 6, 7
word choice, 10, 12, 22, 26, 28

3 1333 05237 4574